To The Reader

This is the work of someone who has tried to gain insight into the growth of his mind by observance of the things that affect it. Therefore, it is neither free of fault, nor oblivious to what it has tried to accomplish, that of setting forth an interpretation of the poetic spirit. These texts were composed during the years 2011-2012 in the silent hours at a desk, or in some instances, in the middle of a field, separate from one another, but all bearing towards that same idea of understanding. This is perhaps why the book will be uninteresting to most, but to those of a reflective nature might such a perusal bring an unexpected vision, or fraternal sentiment, to their off-handed hours, that the reader is not asked to start from the beginning and read to the end, but rather to open the book patiently and find their own way amongst it.

Seasons Of Mind

BOOK I

I. A triumphant day and the warmth of spring! Went searching for edible plants: wild carrot, dandelion, primrose, and speedwell; all blooming, or had bloomed, while still hung the bright red and orange rose-hips telling of winter past.

A dead hedgehog: I had come across the track of this unfortunate creature last autumn, and believing he would have found a burial after so many months, I went in search of him again to see the spot. His barren carcass lay as if the quiet morning of earth was gathering the last few remnants of his life for the final frost of winter--I felt content to find him, and pulling off his quills, put them in my bag to decorate a

---

birch case that I was working on for my knife.

On the 26th of October last this field was very different, and yet these paths and these hills change not as we; the brown mushrooms wilt away, the wheat is mowed down, but our thoughts and our feelings somehow stay the same. Indeed, the seasons force us to change even though it is the last thing we want. The dead oak leaves now tapped each other in the wind as I ate parched corn, the pond was beginning to thaw, the apples were rotting upon the ground, and the hedgehog no longer had his quills.

February 5th, 2011

II. Each event seems to have its season and it is strange to think and conjure up the memory at a different time to the one in which it was first lived. The congenial times with family in winter have not a place in spring or summer; they seem as if asleep, hibernating in the mind, waiting until they again can step out of that deep dark cavern of memory and live, though famished and in need of dire refreshment. Their unseasonableness makes it not that we are happy or sad when they come upon us, rather they wake us with the melancholy thought that the cold and pitiless gusts of our heart have arrived. We cannot walk silently past it, remaining immune to the warmth of a lighted house, nor flee the long fields and forests in perpetual day, but turn again to hibernation, which suddenly, though the rest of us proceed to the new-coming season, searches out the fathoms of our own dark cave.

March 9th, 2011

III. First taste of cattail--a nutty flavor; found some shepherd's purse, chickweed, and stinging nettle, though weak in sting: still an amateur in identifying. There was a pheasant across the field, and now it calls tamely, subtly, as if amongst its kin. We suffer our curiosity to know the names of many plants and animals, yet when come to them in their habitat, on their ground, we refuse their real nature, and they, or we, pass right by. Four young falcons flew above me today and made the strangest calls as they looped around in the air; a sound, truly, I did not think they could make, and it took me more than a moment to look up at the sky, believing the sound was in the far-off hedge.

It is extraordinary to see the old winter paths, or the bedded-down weeds, where the rabbit or field-mouse crossed and waited, then scurried forth for a meal--it is a whole world within itself. There are old plants giving birth to new shoots; and myself, at times, a new thought.

Melancholy teases not so much anymore--I feel I am a poet. I dream, and yet the taste of chickweed tells me I already know it. The land would not be the same without it, and neither I if I strove not for poesy.

A red squirrel ran up not far while I was eating my parched corn and played around, not knowing I was there, then started and ran off--from that alone it feels that I have been known! Wild onion smells everywhere. There were clouds in the morning but the day has turned out nice. I passed an old lady on her back porch, sitting in the sun, who called out to me, 'on chauffe bien!' Going for primrose and then home.

March 11th, 2011

IV. Early on observed a jack-rabbit in the field with my binoculars moving about with a slow gallop here and there, stopping every once in a while to nibble a stalk of grass. The rising sun came up behind him, and it seemed his whiskers hung about in a misty aura.

Came across a dead raven and a dead falcon; the former in a secluded part of a field where no trail lay, and the latter lying across a well-beaten path. Believing them charms of some sort, or wanting indeed to harness some power from the unknown, I cut the head off the raven's dry and shriveled carcass, and took the left claw, some tail feathers, and a right wing feather, from the falcon, as it was fresh, perhaps only a couple days old.

It is often amazing to see death so close, and there is a presentiment that lies about a fresh carcass that says it is still somewhere around, lurking, and if not careful one may be taken along with it--it is enough to make one superstitious, or rather give one the sensation of what life is capable. I felt in taking from the falcon that I should leave something in return, whereon I threw a small pinch of parched corn over his body.

Many questions have come upon me and I have worn a morbid condition for some time now. It is a hassle to know that the season has changed and yet one must remain cooped up in his loft, writing, trying to bring about some sort of poesy--unexpectedness fails after a while and we need the look of death to revitalize us once again. So have I come today, but my questions persist for no other reason than fear of the unexpected.

April 9th, 2011

V. I am beginning to think that morning is for the pure, or those only of the purest souls and truest intent can experience the grace and simplicity that comes from it.   He is born in the morning who dies in the afternoon and it seems we live again and are conscious of our birth.   The many mornings we pass by ourselves, or in the company of the sun, is inspiration: the falcon surveys us, and we follow the paths of rabbit and deer instead of men.

April 10th, 2011

VI. Yesterday morning large towers of clouds coming up from the valley rose through our camp, bringing with it a cool and humid air. Our ascent remained in the clouds and only rarely did we glimpse the large rocks above us, or the massive Alps across the valley to the south.

Today as the sun arose on our hidden and agreeable camp there was a haze amongst the air only adding to the faint mysticism of those mountains.

Last night we made a large fire, and as evening fell away, on the trees around us the small singing birds, quieting their calls, watched from the low branches. Not far a deer became spooked; and as the night wore on, what was believed to be a fox, came lurking around, and from some unperceived spot, watched us a few moments and content, ran off. We, as humans, forget these sounds and are quick to pose them on beings inexistent, or upon men come to do us harm. More often, it is our own breathing we fear, or the wind--truly, nothing is as it seems. For I have witnessed not so long ago just one tiny bird in the underbrush make enough noise for a small group of men, and was actually startled at the occurrence. But we forget that the animals have no fire to warm themselves by, and are much more unaccustomed to that sight than we. However, these sounds tell us what kind of men we were generations ago;

they show our perceptive and ready nature to seek out the unknown; and we all too easily forget that the ground upon which we place our heads was there before our existence.

April 25th, 2011
From La Chartreuse (Plateau des Petites Roches)

VII. The first bird sang this morning at 5:46 am and at this, as I lay in my sleeping bag, listening to the ever-weakening calls of the crickets, and the soft night slowly slip away with the feeble wind, not yet aware of there being a trace of light--as sometimes the brightest days may to the still and contemplative eye seem as approaching night--all the other birds, one by one, began to sing. But as I lay there, telling myself to sleep, a native desire took hold of me to rise to the bird's hearkening. Outside the tent the Dent de Crolles rose above us with a faint and eerie orange shade on its southern face while everything else lay in soft obscurity.

Waited out a storm in the tent last

night. Our camp lay at the end of a meadow, not far from the trail, with a group of tall pines at one end and a sheer drop-off to our right, looking south. We could see the waves of rain off in the valley, and waited the storm from that direction, but it snuck up on the other side, coming over the Dent de Crolles with a burst of wind and loud thunder.

Through each successive hiking trip every former trip is relived. There is always a landscape, a smell in the breeze, a rock, something that reminds us of our days long past, which leads us further into a journey we have yet taken.

April 26th, 2011
From La Chartreuse (Plateau des Petites Roches)

VIII. Found some mint, wild mustard, red clover, white clover, and took some wild rosebuds for a tea.

Is it that man cannot say when he would be most intimate? He may hear the butterflies land upon the leaves of grass; spiders leap from stalk to stalk; flies, bees, and all insects make a quieter and contemplative chorus than the birds; the hare crack a stick in the bush; the lizard dive out of the crevices of rocks, but I another song myself, and one they know is not natural--I am a stranger today.

I wonder if my footsteps will integrate this grand nature; or, truly, if I will ever step as light as those, hear as soft as they, and speak with them who never utter words. How should I be understood--how should I be intimate if not! None can refuse this sentiment, just as none, if they know who they are, can follow any other, but must, unto a lonely pasture full of wildflowers, become the path he has led himself on.

Passed a field today where the hares had been eating yellow goat's beard.

May 4th, 2011

A place beside wild chamomile
Where rabbits often hide....

IX. The farmers started their haying at the beginning of the week and some have already begun taking up their bales. The field mustard is almost head high, some higher; and wild chamomile and wild geranium have appeared as if on the moment.

Found out a small, secluded field, and by slow and awkward movements the birds, frightened at my approach, have begun to return to the hedgerows to sing. It is windy today, but in the thickets of wild rose the bird's nest seems a place of whimsical comfort. The sun shines and there are high clouds--in the distance the atmosphere looks dirty.

I have come to realize that we must not search the ideal: disappointment will always follow. It is that we must follow our instinct and by this come to our ideal. As I was struggling through a large patch of briars earlier, stopping constantly to ask myself if I should go on, suddenly a serene pasture wooded by old mishapen pines opened up before me. The wonderful scent of those trees, and the sheer desolation of coming upon an unknown piece of land, gave to this scene an almost surreal sentiment. I know not if I saw the same things, nor heard the same sounds, as someone else would have. Anywhere, as long as it was under those pines, seemed an intention or a dream that wasted, by the light of the sun, so many looks and gestures into thin air, or on bare spots of ground, at once enchanted by solitude and at another befuddled at its enchantment. I laughed when I had thought, midway through those low thickets, to turn back. Found an old and damaged falcon wing, perhaps picked clean by a fox.

These days of solitude have been a burden and a freedom; the burden I know not, the freedom because I've overcome what I know not, and so who I am, what I long to be, and in my mind room for the ages.

May 7th, 2011

X. The morning was autumnal in a sort. The wind blew cold, the sky was grey, and the fields had a strange appearance of suffering from a long summer. I am not sure why I desire to see the sky grey, the trees no longer green, and a perfect desolation upon the fields. The seasons change, or so our perception of it, and time is transcended, leaving us to create each sentiment from the dark remains of the land before us, though it is we only fool ourselves.

We often say that he acts like him or her, or much resembles them, but little do we say he acts as the weather or resembles a field; yet it is no less true, whether imagination solely acts upon our exterior world to cause these phenomena, making us the true bearers of our fortune and fate, or scientifically we reason out and prove why in the month of May we may feel the solitudes of autumn. Montaigne says that man can only be as great as himself, and therein never reaching perfection, why should it be considered that what he lays down as truth and reason beyond doubt not be tainted by what he himself is ever struggling to get past. What we perceive as reality is truthful only to the mood in which we find ourselves at the moment: I resemble the field only as much as I take care to observe it. Other dreams and other reasons shall let he who wants declare what is just and profound, what is strict and unchanging, and what is, by all means the ever present truth that many ages and many experiments have proven. Aside from that, there is still something human, there is still a real belief that what is, is not, and what has yet to be will never come. The world outside of my heart and mind is solely dependent on my footstep wherever it is placed at that moment. I do not believe the world revolves for me, but in its revolution I take part, and only when the world ceases will I. Autumn is ever present alongside the other seasons, and when it rains the sun still shines high up in the air.

Found an abundance of chamomile, mint, yarrow, and a plant called pineapple weed, of a scent that brought me in direct contact with my childhood, as I think it grew on the margins of the gravel road in front of our first house. Wild grape has flowers on the stem and the hawthorn berries are green. The wild-strawberry patch that I had marked out has succumb to blight. For the first time I am trying to make a soothing oil from st. john's wort. Also gathered contacts for picking fruit this summer.

May 16th, 2011

XI. Fruit-picking season has started and I am determined to find work before the day is through. Sitting in an abandoned cabin waiting on a storm to pass; light rain and thunder have filled the sky with a faint desolation that rules my time in this small forgotten room with the ancient and hapless wanderings of lost men. I believe I could inhabit such a place: wheat fields abounding on each side, only a trail to the front door; there is room enough for a stove, a bed, a table, perhaps a radio, no running water though. As I look out the door into the long distant fields, hazy with rain, I can imagine myself the owner; I can feel myself the guard and overseer of those few and unstressing tasks for which the simple life binds one to the days and weeks. Such was living, that for want of rest or too much rain, man found himself out some quiet and lonely spot where his fears and apprehensions could retreat for a while, and upon these became his towns and cities. What terror, though, when upon some nights, and in some storms, he found himself in a place where he could not rest--what places have those become? Do we not walk upon them today still with a certain uneasiness and anxious imagination?

Even here, there are the ruins of a Roman aqueduct barely a quarter of a mile off, hidden and overgrown, and perhaps unknown to most of the inhabitants around. House upon house has been built, and so, man: what Roman or Gaul before me sat here, working out Cato's farming books or studying Frontinus' work on water supply? Would he not have walked in this light rain and thunder, appeased of the fact that here he lives, and here he may withstand the powers of nature, while another, less sure, would shield himself from it? Would it be too strange to consider that that other could be what he once had dreamed and will soon return to antiquity? I know not; for we shall never dream as we live, and those thoughts we finally attain always seem to be the men we shall never be.

May 20th, 2011

XII. I have come to realize that what seems to give me the most pleasure is not the object itself, but the memory connected with it, so that the many hours passed in front of something only hold profit by the many hours being away from it. My joy is only joy in dissolution and the dream but never more real and truthful than when awake. What chimeras I create from what I have experienced gather not by longing for some melancholic sort of image the greater part of the day in mourning, but is held in a perpetual state of neither fleeing nor observing my daily thoughts, as a background to which my frame of mind takes comfort. Some days I find myself angry for a slight that happened some weeks past, or give I thanks and grant appreciation for something which I was extremely dull towards only a matter of hours ago, but their importance, whether it comes now or some years from now, is a beacon to reflection--the matter dies not though time may fade away. These moments, then, that from poetry I shall be away, and voluntarily cede that time to fruit-picking, are now for me, even in its anticipation, a sort of renaissance and new spring.

May 23rd, 2011

XIII. Perhaps it is a great weakness of contemplation when our hours of thought cede to irreconcilable difficulties and take small accord in our efforts if they are not gained by drudgery. I tend not with composure to pursue or conduct any sort of undertaking with a heed to be repugnant--it lingers away until the idea is no longer frightening and I pick up again my efforts with less indecision and a relief of mind that is forgiving to jobs well done. If I have not suffered and a thought comes out unpoetic and the words ephemeral, how much more difficult it is to be pleasing and kind-hearted, but how much more certain will the mind do away with what is artificial and laugh at the human for nothing else than what he has been taught to do, if only but to see into the genuine art of his condition. Scorn, anger, ignorance, are all but fronts to something deeper, to something that poetry has not yet attained, to something that fails not the condition, but the human. What he speaks is the falsity of fools and what he presents is a consolation to his heart; for the lengthy roads down which the mind may travel are narrow and leave little room for outside judgement. He is sad, weary, and yet unmoved; hated, absurd, and yet attentive; all the world is but a fleeting touch, and when accomplished, dreams of no better end.

May 25th, 2011

XIV. Spinoza spoke truth when he said the immediate understanding of our world comes from the experiences in which we have lived. There is a serenity in the repetitive wherein no truth or human mind, but balance between languor and activity, is a means to perpetual happiness; and there are few seldom immune to those interior connections that are refreshed daily by the dawn of day, or the smell of dirt and leaves, or the taste of fruit upon a tree; nor be they immune to any sadness or melancholy but what comes through the realization and termination of their daily work with the setting of the sun. He is a man above a man that can overcome the petty distractions of his inner life and reach out into the further spheres, knowing that he is the relation and purpose of thought in the world. To undertake that work, once immersed, or subjected to the idea, every thought that passes, which is blind to daily life, has a layered meaning within the work itself: the work in us speaks for the work that we must do.

June 4th, 2011

XV. One may say that in the field today he listened to a bird, and his life, for an instant, sounds poetic. He pays homage to those things all of us pass by, but he shall only be poetic for a day and should there come a time when he immerse himself in the poetic character, to take the brunt of a hard look and grim silence, to hear him say aloud that in the field he searches for plants, and watches the insects gather round, and the bird, when it sings, he looks up in the trees, and if he find it not, he sees it in his mind, and listens, as he would a poem; then he may be prepared for the majestic solitude that upbuilds the body, takes away all worry, and lets us proceed to ourselves. The poetic character comes not by one's interaction with his fellow man, but in his emotion to the nature that surrounds him. He steps away from man to see him from a distance, but only then to make himself man: for it is here, the difference, should he be ready to be himself or another. Prepare then for loneliness and disappointment, for these are what give us our company and hope.

June 7th, 2011

XVI. The more we associate certain places with the ideals in our mind the more they become them, or the more the ideal is effaced for reality, so that the things from which we hide, or those upon which our comforts have grown, bear an intimacy to that which has turned from them, and what we thought unbelievable in us to conceive, is now the means by which we understand our memories.

There was a painting that I had known in my youth hanging upon the mantle of our childhood home, showing a cottage in an overgrown field with an old tree above it, and in the clouds--at least to the imagination--there was the form of a lady leaning upon the air. In youth, perhaps, we adjudge too much of the magical, and scenes of fabled splendour, that in later times will be looked upon nonchalantly; for I know not if that painting is truly as whimsical as I remember, but something from it has, and perhaps always will, guided me to the highest vaults of inspiration. And yet, in another land, and of another culture, so far from reconciling it with a true habitation, there is some part of me that has found a certain similarity in the land almost parallel to what it had shown. As I came to my habitual spot in the field to eat my parched corn and rest from picking cherries, I saw my imprint in the grass from the day before, and that painting of my childhood suddenly appeared to me, and for the first time did I understand the importance of feeling at home.

June 8th, 2011

XVII. I know not if exterior joys are sufficient for the happiness of mankind; for what the individual sees, and takes care to provide himself with, seems not to have them as its greatest end. Certainly the beginnings we undertake show not the same end, or if so, choose not to reveal it so clearly--no one thinks logically when they see the light of the sun upon the distant hills mark the strange and interior beauties of their lives. We foresee greater comforts though it be no further or deeper than the surrounding atmosphere.

Is it possible to be happy in one place, to come upon it each time as if it were renewed, or there were a season unknown to us? Where does that ever-renewing presence hide that turns the trees a lighter shade of green, that makes the breeze bring different odours, and changes our perception, not upon distant lands, but upon the same lands distant? Again to this spot of ground I've come that now I know so well, that has given me past memories and relaxation; and yet today, it is no more than a place that I have come to many times, a place where I have seen the same things over and over, a place too close to spying eyes, too close to the village, and I look away from it as if I might find somewhere else. A wilder spot would perhaps give me momentary comfort but I know not if I could sincerely give myself up to it: for would I not search the same things that now I search in this spot? Perpetual choice has always been a bane to my humour, to know that anything, whatever it is, is never settled, to know that happiness is fleeting, and the spot upon which we find our comforts an ever-changing moment in the light of day.

June 9th, 2011

XVIII. 'Another day,' I find myself saying, 'tomorrow I will go here', 'in an hour or so I must do this': these expressions are always closest to my mind, yet I feel they bring nothing but dissent. We may be as sturdy in heart as the oak, but when I am under its shade and spreading branches, I am as evasive as the wind when it fills the upper canopy, swaying back and forth. It leads to a frank and strange emotion that tells me where I am is not where I should be, or what I think upon is not the only thing I should ponder. 'I must not linger,' I say, 'I must give the body work, see what is over the further hill,'--and yet, in all this, I am very lazy. The sentiment which lives in the present is always fleeting, always before or after us, and yet there is but a moment of clarity which makes us aware that we hold on to something.

I take the flower or the leaf up in hand, and as I turn it into the light, or the wind lifts it awkwardly, I hold anything but what my mind thinks it is: the flower leaves to my later engagements troubles and worries; to my former actions, doubt and uncertainty; the leaf, the bird, or the bee, my departure from this grassy solitude; for they are not feelings which have a place until I see the buds of the hawthorn, or the sloe-berry first appear, but so far are they from those shades of indifference, that when I see them, I am happy.

June 17th, 2011

XIX. I have found myself to the art of cherry picking a quiet observer. Pierre, the old man who runs the orchard, will empty a branch of cherries, perhaps 10 feet long, without moving his bucket or bringing his hands down from the tree. He has a certain way of guiding the cherries, when his hands become too full, to fall directly where he wants them; and the only thing that remains to the observer is a melody of faint thuds. I have a few times started on a branch the same as him, when in the mornings he would walk amongst us and begin his picking on some out of the way tree so as to show us our direction for the rest of the day; and though I were among the fastest or most determined of the workers, his bucket would be filled though mine were only half or a little more full.

At lunch, I sat and watched the rays of sun fall down through a hedge out in the field, until they reached a newly sprouted hawthorn sapling in the underbrush, leaving everything else around it in somber shade--this was when I knew it was time for me to return to work.

June 21st, 2011

XX. While watching a group of swifts glide back and forth in the sky with an apparently strange urge of necessity, there came on with slow and steady wing amidst them a falcon with unconcerned grace. For a moment, he flew among them seemingly unnoticed, but as his flight became more direct, or as he was finally recognized as a stranger, a few of those smaller birds turned suddenly, and flying close upon his tail, heckled him for some distance. The broad expanse of the falcon's wings began taking up a more urgent flight, and his body twisting and turning to avoid the agility of the swifts, proved quite a comical spectacle for such a majestic bird, and pity, not for the victors, but for the ruthless one defeated, passed over me, though I could not help but smile.

I have seen the same activity in magpies as well. These birds will suddenly shoot out from the middle of some unexpected tree whenever the first sign of a falcon comes to them, and making straight for him in a fast but undulating flight, raise a great cry, so that the falcon, though at first very unconcernedly, changes his flight, just as he does with the swifts, twisting and turning his body, trying to gain as much speed as possible. The magpies will trail him for some distance, picking at his feathers, the falcon offering no signs of resistance; and if one may see to the horizon, when the two birds finally part, the falcon as if he had not been flustered, and the magpie labouring with all energy to get back to his tree, it is in itself no wonder that the common ground upon which things find their accord are only for an instant triumphant and must constantly reassert themselves if they are ever to gain any importance.

June 30th, 2011

XXI. The most pleasurable of moments come not when we are engaged with dreams and contemplation, but when, through the hazard of living, we become fully lost to ourselves and are led, not by whims or slow deduction, but by an interest that is revealed only to us. I may spend the greater part of my days deciding for what reason and in what place I have come here or sat there or have taken this path instead of that one, or wanted to pass by the creek instead of the hill, and yet the satisfaction that I get from these decisions equals in no way the pleasure I get if I had stayed home and lost myself to study, or had been led through books and encyclopedias in search of a name or a quote that for some reason had taken hold of me.

Too often are we forced to move ourselves instead of being moved; we believe ourselves better for planning the day, nobler if we have things to do, but the foundations of men begin to crumble when they no longer have the momentum of choice: the character of a man is seen only when he is moved by that which he cannot see nor has decided to see. He is greater than us all who lets himself be moved not by devotion to one thing, nor the emotion of one event, but by the exterior simplicity of the world in which he lives, and of those decisions not taken, or truthfully, inexistent.

July 1st, 2011

XXII. There are two hills to the north, rising from the lake at Mornant, and so thoroughly had I walked across the plains that lead up to them, that I started to long for new scenery. My walks had become too comfortable, and the forests and habitations that I would see from afar, rather than taking my journey to them, urged me to lay in the grass and wonder, and soon disappoint myself, as to such an undertaking. I had always known the village of St. Martin-En-Haut lay beyond those hills--I had been there, had walked upon the trails, and always with the same disappointment decided against linking one village to the other because I knew not the way: the fear of going down the wrong path, though docile and miniscule, turned me upon the broader prospects of comfort and safety. And yet, becoming more resolute to the idea, I set out one morning with the intention of fulfilling my plans, and no sooner had I left St. Martin bound for Mornant did I return unknowingly to the former village by a path that I thought led away from it. My disappointment redoubled, not through failure, but lack of will; I had reached the heights of those two hills, could see the lake, and yet it was all mysteriously distant, not by land, but in mind.

Today I set out again from St. Martin, and though I fell a victim to the same fault, I was able to correct it by looking the other way, by going in a 'wrong' direction. I felt myself the whole day further and further away from where I needed to go. I looked suspiciously upon the trees and recognized neither landmark nor variation in the scenery. But to my surprise, just before seeing a snake on the shaded path crawl off into the creek, a strange perception came over me, as if I had seen into a new world, and I realized that I were walking on a path that I knew. Emerson says that it is sufficient to turn ourselves upside down and look at the landscape which is familiar to us so that we may see it newly: a different direction changes what we know though the path be well-worn. But to pass a place we once have been, and have yet to recognize, is perhaps one of the calmest and gentlest feelings I have ever witnessed. Now those rolling meadows which I had passed earlier, though I did not admire them, hold a certain sweetness because they are connected with what I know, and had always known.

July 8th, 2011

XXIII. There is not a season for raspberries; they seem to get picked soon enough. On the days the weather was bad we were sent off to the greenhouse to pick them, but for the most part, everyday from the end of May until the beginning of July was spent with the cherries. When it rains hard enough, you don't pick; and there were days when I would look to the sky and see a thunder-cloud off in the distance, hoping that it would come our way, though I hated not what I was doing. Rain and thunder are a pleasing break to the bird's song and the fly's buzz, and even the relaxing motions of restrained labour profit by haste. To the first drops of rain have so many words lent themselves that upon its arrival we

---

cannot but feel that somewhere deep inside of us one of our most secret and unknown hopes has been met.

We finished the season by picking red-currants, a somewhat tedious job as the clusters are for the most part hidden around the branches, and the bushes being not so tall, provide no relief from the sun. We finished around mid-day, then Pierre invited us across the road to his house where lunch had been prepared. We ate of pheasant pâté, raspberry sorbet, and drank of walnut liqueur. In the weeks before, I had made known my preference for these 'wild' liqueurs, those made from fruits growing uncultivated in the field, and on my leaving, Pierre handed me a jar of griotte liqueur--a type of sour cherry mixed with alcohol--and thereon my days as a cherry-picker ended. I spent the rest of the day in an old out of the way field where wild plum trees grew and, though it seemed odd, I noticed, as I lay in the grass and looked up to the sky, the falcon and the butterfly together in flight.

July 11th, 2011

XXIV. What we believe to be our pre-destined path shall lead and nourish us by an understanding which we vaguely comprehend. Sympathy is hard to find in such a situation and even harder so to dress in natural sentiment. What is different holds in it just that which we cannot reckon genuine--we are put off by it and it seems more a master over us than what we know and what we hold as truth, so that what is false gives us a greater perception into what we believe of it. When it comes down to feeling or acting upon what we know, those first few steps are foreign, strange, until it is that we have effaced all indifference. The sun will rise but not I to my duty unless I feel I have overcome that which gives me disdain--I am happy only by my shortcomings, though what joy I feel in them is latent and at times misconstrued. Left unto himself, man errs not but by his own capacity, which if he look to it, is but the base of an institution and higher reform upon which he is master; for, amongst the many, he errs by all of those who have claimed from another that same title.

July 29th, 2011
Started trek in the Pyrénées

XXV. With these I see the past events go by: the hill that leads up to the pass, the echoing of the cow-bells across the field, and the horses swaying gently through the day. The terrain is faintly mountainous, yet there is an aura that subtly speaks of these things in the wind. One looks up with expectation to find his view dashed by the trees or the long sloping hill and he is far from his imagination, yet wherever there is a respite in the leaves, or the earth abruptly falls into the sky, there is something of anticipation and an urge to move on. Some think that with every new view there comes profound inspiration, that we are fulfilled by the grandeur of Nature, and what our eyes look upon speaks the intention that the heart demands; but he comes with old steps unto those undiscovered places and his surprise or astonishment is a reminiscence of the long experience that has led him back to his childhood.

July 30th, 2011
Massif du Pibeste

XXVI. We awoke to a cold and breezy morning; for the sun had not as yet eclipsed the high summits and its light only shown faintly on the western slopes. The serene feeling of waking up in the sunken depths of a mountainous valley, and the whole surrounding space but silent and calm, contents one with an activity of mind alert to the most passive of moments--but it is cold.

We begin to wonder how important the sun is to the maintenance of health and sound mind, and speak of the cold and the wind in jest, because down the slope, tree by tree, the sun comes closer: the mind that was once empty is full and he who awakes from difficult sleep becomes soothed. He conquers and lives in the dawning light, but has only seen and felt the sun, and once the morning is gone, he seeks out shades and quiet dwellings to pass the better part of light and warmth in tired resolutions. Too innocent be our hopes, for they flee upon first light; are lulled to perdition by a certain warmth of heart, and when they see fall the final rays of the sun, relief and the cool soothing air come once again to comfort us. We turn upon the night as if by the flame of some new and ever-protecting fire, but too quickly the cold returns.

August 10th, 2011
Néouvielle

XXVII. Below us, as we climbed further and further to a point above the lake, the fish that were once hidden in the depths, or the reflection of the water, came forth one by one through the rays of the sun, until the whole bank, and thus floating away from it, was filled with the slow meandering and brief pause of their movements. Rising further, we looked back upon them; the lake again became opaque, and the bank, at the nearest reception of water, ceded to the blue and profound reflection of the whole.

August 11th, 2011
Lac de l'Oule

XXVIII. This morning as I leaned against a rock in the pale of dawn, the soft flame and subtle heat of the sun grew upon my back, as if some giant overstepping the valley, and on the ground in front of me, against the increasing light, my shadow appeared within the very air of which a moment before gave no semblance of human being. The grandeur, or the deep, profound obscurity of things, that lay hidden in the mellow breath of time, wherein the center of our universe comes to completion, and the most important point of that now-revolving cycle of life and death no longer exists, are the moments, of which we so desperately hold on to, that pass into the shallow beams of eternity.

August 12th, 2011

XXIX. The fire that we made in the evening light to warm ourselves, or to give attention to an erring mind, was, with the little wood gathered from around us, a fair impression from which to take repose and enjoy the difficulties of the day. The sky drew to a close its blue and settling light, and the sun about to peek its last, as the flames withered away into the air, giving unto the eye, as it glanced back and forth from fire to empty space, the bold colours of evening. The moon arose, large, and tainted with a shade of the mountainous horizon, and at one time, between the sun, the fire, and the moon, it was no more to speak of the difficulties of the day, but the veiled and changing dimensions of night.

August 13th, 2011

XXX. What terminated the night with rain left us in the morning with a view upon which we could see the last summits of our trek before the interminable descent into the trees and rigid slopes. Gave they some satisfaction, the sky upon which we left our zeal served with a place and origin to renewal and further achievement, and at last, an idea from which we took some image of beauty. The man may become a mountain, but the mountain will not become a man and the intrigues from which he scales those heights are upon his descent the pleasures and the habits with which he leads himself back to reality. Returns he again to the place he camped, sees he again the trail he took, he is ever met with that same stern regard that says he can only go so far, only do so much, and herein lies the summit of his existence and his pain. He looks once more upon this scene, then turns his bewildered look to the rest of mankind: he is a stranger, a friend of the inanimate, and ever and again into what low valley he may, the lost, and soon inconceivable mountains, are a partner to his intimate thoughts.

August 14th, 2011
End of trek in the Pyrénées

XXXI. Is not memory the image that we give to space? All of what we see is past and all of what is past be that dimension with which we see. While looking upon the trees or into the horizon, I cannot help but reflect upon those things long gone from me. The familiarity of the birds are in my mind what I think of it, not what it is. We watch ourselves play in the sunlight--they are mere jests; what we see is not what we feel and what we feel is only imagined, so that as we reflect, we remember not that past events go by, but live again. All of what is contained within our minds is the sky, the stars, and the space of what we remember; we fill every corner of it with humble origin.

August 16th, 2011

XXXII. How far the feather flies that helps not soar the eagle's wing! Passed the orchard, now bare, where I spent the spring and summer picking cherries. The low trees still looked ravaged, as if our hands had just passed over them, and the silence, of what was once interminable days of heat and sweat, held the most pleasant desolation. We could pass among the rows at liberty, and I could point to spots and specific days with only the weight of memory as a friend, to prove with what indolence or joy the long hours had passed. But pride, or the simple pretension of not doing enough, or from the solemn mysteries that lead away the human heart from what is done, bore not a path upon which my steps could turn.

We took leisure among the red-currants close by to fill our bags, and this, added to the raspberries and blackberries, gave us quaint retreat in the adjacent fields to look over our harvest, and speak of fondness and the loss of temporary friends.

August 21st, 2011

XXXIII. There is a tree upon the edge of a clearing in Vaugneray, much away from the sight of men--and perhaps for this reason more affecting--that at the first commencement of the fall season, its leaves begin to change, from whence the other trees seem to take heed. I believe it last year when I first noticed this, or when I gave unique appearance to the demeanor and habitation of certain trees and their association with the season--for what unbelievable feeling is expressed in our acknowledgement of change and our perseverance in affection, be they but the quiet mark of dreams or the slow receding light of evening.

The sight had so affected me that

thereafter, when all the leaves had fallen and winter arrived, I anticipated for many months the season of autumn, claiming at the first browning of any tree, though it were dead or diseased, that the season was upon us. I had no hope if only but to gain an extra day, or moment, in seeing nature unawares show its hidden face, and spent, as if in languishment, the whole next summer in this manner. As I ventured out this morning, my sole hope was to find again this tree, and coming upon it, I felt with some sort of humanly distinction, relief, and even a profound sadness, at seeing the leaves once more their furtive essence show. I sat before it, whereon a breeze arose and blew downwards through the fainting sky what first few leaves had turned from the green of summer's light their affected origins. The coolness of the air drew a shiver from the trees and from myself, and in a moment, nothing more had I to look forward to.

September 2nd, 2011

XXXIV. The tediousness of losing a thought provokes in us the anxiety of much worse. Often in the most tranquil hours have I been caught by the need to remember some off-handed subject or idea, that I begin to ask the subtle forms and dying whims of recent musing what it is that must delineate my frame of mind into reticence. But the response that comes carries my imagination to the wild and scary conjectures of past events, so as to give what is not there advantage over what is most real. And to declare this or that definitive at such a moment tends rather to take away confidence from a creative nature and fill the mind with a lack of authentic sentiment, so that the light that shines in the morning becomes the softest approach by which to guide it back to dreaming. But worst of all, once we begin to believe this, all our thoughts recline in cheap opinion.

September 20th, 2011

XXXV. Very rarely, when the dreams of night have all but dissipated their timid charms, will I be awoken by a word or sentence so delicate, so touching the borders of my conscious activity and pursuit, that the failing constraints of light sleep become released, and I am seized by the urgency of a word giving a long sought solution to that idea, or to that passage, which difficulty let not my waking hours construct. But the febrility with which I accept it, though I know it is from some deep region of mind wherein fancy holds but the utmost pains to break through, is filled with a restrictive sentiment, so that before I am fully aware and ready to steal upon my pen and write it down, the clarity and innocence of the expression begins to vanish, and there is nought but my grasping through the faint darkness a specious image from what was once its own entity.

This morning, the loss of one such expression as it awoke me from sleep, brought a contrariety into my mind from which I have not yet recovered, and feel the whole day will be lost in vain seeking and startled turns of thought, instead of the brave exploration with which it had inspired and undertook my dreams and first waking moments. Were I ever to get back to that fair-looking meadow, and the world with which my mind has sought to prove, would my attention find in constant languor those adornments that often give us means to bring forth truth.

September 22nd, 2011

XXXVI. I wonder how much our demeanor depends upon our birth and that time of year, and what changes come to pass, oblivious to us, wherein some pensiveness, languor, or sadness, has been attributed too wrongly to an event, when it was but the stirrings of the inner heart which had sent us into our doom. We step upon the curb and lose our balance, but it is not the fault of our foot, nor the curb; there is a deep cycle of inward motion which submits not to reason. Everyday we are of a different disguise and a part of the human who walks as the ancient Sumerian, smiles as Plato, and holds his pen as a medieval scribe. I do not believe in time's perpetual forward motion, but think it scattered among objects and physical presence, so that, as all lies beyond it is mystery, the thoughts and the world to which we constrain ourselves, only allow us those things familiar to our surroundings. Even he who lives farthest from us is as a neighbor, and before coming into our company, we already imitate him inwardly. The individual exists not, yet he may, at times, find himself alone and separated. Last week I was sad, and all of my actions held a grandeur I could not regain, but now they are so foreign, that I know not if it were me who undertook them.

September 24th, 2011

XXXVII. 'Where nature's form helps not the end intelligence alights.' Throughout the day these words came back to me, yet I know not where I heard them. There is a strange inspiration, of which Nietzsche speaks, that comes as lightning, that makes one speak though he know not why or where the urge comes from. We have in us something so invariably poetic that I think the duty of daily life be to suppress this, to pull out all of the unknown, not that we may be so undeniably common, but to give the impression of uniqueness and herald reward into the light of day. Madness is forever appealing, it is what permits change; we look to it as submission to an ideal. Yet if we all search to reveal the tyrant motion of the soul, do we not force ourselves into that false image from which madness takes its form? The moment we know, illusion ceases, and those things we hope for, and desire, be not of naive intentions. I know not why the normal finds itself in the abnormal, and intelligence through ignorance, but it proves experience so very far from understanding, that it is close to the ideas we sometimes seek. We cannot find the Muses, nor accord their habitation. Yet, of all the millions of things that have now entered the mind and passed, how long must it take for this inspiration to strike again; how long must it be before we hear again ourselves; and who then, when it comes, will we be?

September 27th, 2011

XXXVIII. 'Each day one becomes more patient, each day he succeeds in wisdom.' Yet I think this needs clarification. We tend to lose patience faster than it is acquired, and it is no surprise that what resists our attempts should receive our condemnation. But what is worthy of our attention should be worthy of our respect, though attention lead us into such great misunderstandings that before we know the thing that attends us, we hate it. Therefore, attention is already filled with so many prejudices that when we believe ourselves with clear mind to understand and define some difficulty, we have transferred the idea upon something else, to give us respite, wherein we take hold of reason instead of facing ignorance. To be oblivious may appease some, but if we accept fate with indifference then intelligence comes at the price of accepting only that which it can answer, and to that which it cannot, impatience, prejudice, and spite. The triumph may only be had when we feel the emotions with which we have been endowed go beyond their moralistic principle; and so, what we support in patience is won through all that is contrary to the moment, even if that moment holds in its weight eternity.

October 6th, 2011

XXXIX. When I am far from men, I believe them all too quickly on the trail of my thoughts. For I am paralyzed by the chimeras of their actions, knowing the outcome before they have well taken a step to create it. In this, at the center of my thoughts, lie the laws and reasons that entrap my will: the leaves may fall, but it is no good should they be of a colour I have not anticipated. I choose a book, but turn past all the pages because the idea does not speak to me. In every act, there is a past which the sullen heart fears, and the bland generality of its climax--the stability, habit, and reasoning--leaves a future that is already condemned to suffer our most boring and nonchalant intentions. I fear most heartily that future that the past is ever so willing to give us; I fear the beginning because there is forever connected to it an end, and I sulk in the thoughts of men who see me walking in the street and despair that what they think will always tell me what will be.

October 11th, 2011

XL. When anxiety hangs about us and tells of some evil, let it be taken lightly lest a greater evil befall. Our undertakings are less susceptible if we do not give them cause or unreal superiority over that which we think will forever be--time gives unequal truth to the past, and to the future a forever narrowing opinion of what everyday shall happen. I have lately seen my views change in the most dangerous manner, from that freedom of spirit which talks of fate with courageous fatality, into the man who sees every circumstance and consequence a condemning mark upon the forest leaves. Be it age, be it the effects of solitude, vulnerability has unmasked its face with swollen eyes and sees behind every charm a twofold expanse of suspicion: one fleeing and one becoming. The happiest moments leave a desire and longing to return to those realms which no longer exist, to ask of them reason, but what is received is foul and unhealthy. And so I forget to act and fear speaks as a sickness, and the comfort of lying in bed all day brings with it a certain pleasure.

November 7th, 2011

XLI. How a simple problem entangles despair and can dishearten to the point that in any book or to any person the answer will be searched, though it only require a fraction of the time in contemplation to convince itself of a solution. Power and the superior might of overcoming has never been for me a truly human feature: the step forward was made by chance, work moved along only by less resistance--it was the problem which defeated itself. Helpless redemption always seems the most logical outcry, that when all hope is lost, one will see a certain uniformity of presence from which his despair had blinded him before: the luckless walks and the fruitless whinings would give account for what at some time in the future would fit me with a more conducive destiny. The world would end before I cede my pride and give out my knowledge as cheap! But I have no desire to seek what I know and for any problem send off to any other source but myself--and this is the addiction: telling others what others know, but know not yourself. And this is terror: knowing the problem is only yours and no other's.

November 21st, 2011

XLII. There is a dread which slowly builds upon the eve of such events wherein our hope is placed, and hoists us between two contraries, as if our excitement, knowing of its mutability, becomes too weak to vanquish the sturdiness of fear. That moment, though it is shrouded in a certain mystery, seems to me a comfort, not because my pleasure is at once extinguished and I become conscious of my vulnerability, but because the changing perception of the event leaves me with a stern conviction that the mundanities of the world, and all of that which to us has become common, hold in them an omnipresent power which our fear makes us at once aware: fear tells us that nothing is common, that everything is possible. However, by nature, we are ever at a variance with the unknown, with the future; it is forever something that will amaze us, but however so much it may make us muse, and the common and mundane trials of life bring us, and set for us, the limits of our consciousness, preference will always lie with the latter: fear and despair will ever be an evil. The poet, in his moment of inspiration, never fears the unknown, and is forever in pursuit of residing with it.

December 4th, 2011

XLIII. There is more solitude in knowing where man has lived and lives no more than where we know he has never lived. That which once was of great importance and held the attentions and thoughts of prior men, yet in our day gets but a passing look, brings the greatest compliment and relief I can give to my mind. The trees and the forest paths are only pretensions if I know they were made and cut out of the ground for my pleasure; the sound of the birds, the wind, and even the cold itself, become oddities or get smeared away to indifference and lose every breath of mystic quality. But when they rise from the ground sacred and with the intention of depth, how large the rose-hip or the hickory nut acclaim their significance. Each step becomes the chanting of a song; my look, at every turn, falls upon the earthen walls, as they linger in and out of sunlight, holding the younger shadows of the rising trees with a long meandering melancholy. Whatever haze or hidden patch of frost remains, has a listless dream of eternity so finely shrouded into the air or blades of grass, that I think myself vain for looking, and lapse in and out of some insensitive world, confused by simple myth. These are brief, and the sun is but a harsh reminder of our impatience, and I turn from them as if I were sent away.

December 11th, 2011
Fort Ancient

XLIV. I've realized for the first time how the sycamore whitens in colour as we look up to the top of its branches. From the edge of the cliff I could see the effect for miles on the surrounding hills--light, faint, ever-vanishing into the winter haze. For it is well to see some ancient work of art, but even more so to look away from it, to see what it sees. When all of our attention lies upon the thing perceived, too often do we miss the full realization: we stare at what attracts us but abuse what has attracted it.

We took the trail that leads down to Brush Creek for the first time, where I found a red rock lying among the damp earth of a newly dug-out burrow. The surprise took me with such unreal expectancy that I seized it with avid vigour, jealous not of what I had, but what else I might get; for our first expectation rises not with how close we understand the object, but how true the object accords to our expectations. I hoped only of what I could not see; of long-lost caves, old fishing camps, the lone deer; for I walked as the intrepid hunter and looked upon the most normal and commonplace pasture as if I were seeing the foundations of an old village. But as I settled down, and the first excitement died off, I looked again to that rock--that worthless, worthless rock--yet could not let it fall from my grip.

December 19th, 2011
Serpent Mound

BOOK II

I. That which is dearest hides in the phantoms of the mundane; and what is left in despair is found again with distinction. The buds from which the forest leaves are drawn looked the same to the Romans and the Gauls; and the acorn is no different from those at home. There are in this territory trees that seem old enough for Caesar to have leaned against, but that remarkable link of fulfillment, that burning comprehension of life, remains behind a shade of mystery. We search in all things refreshment, a fantasy of the past, for it is not their exterior natures but the imagination within which they are held that give us a way to existence. The growth is not in us but through us; we are the difference of two opposing spheres, the world in which we think we are, and the one that we create.

January 2nd, 2012

II. From what truly great thing may we take our example? Are we condemned to rise above us that which is only plain and simple, and by giving to it our will, turn it into the ideal from which inspiration feeds? The further I search for that most honourable and rare trait in life, the more my imagination fumbles with things which are below it, and tend to pull attention away. Sir Thomas Browne said that the greatness of a thing lies in its modesty; for the grandeur of something is weighed by the undertaking, and those which surpass our comprehension, or which are sufficient in themselves, ultimately fail in producing a greater effect. It is not the falling light of day which is beautiful, nor the song of a morning bird when all is quiet; their greatness lies not in our amazement or our disregard, but in us building them into our character. The man who is great has something of the unexpectedness and familiarity of a song-bird, and when he undertakes his affairs, there is spread over him a falling light.

January 13th, 2012

III. Heard for a moment (11:54am) the song of a bird of spring, the black-bird--it is sunny, but the air is cold, and the temperature below zero. It never fails in the solitudes of dying winter, to bring me out of my slumber, hearing the echo of a creature with a nature dissimilar to mine. There are things which hold silence in making noise, just as if dreams could hold truth in waking from sleep, but still the bird sings to the realms of our most distant charms. How different is our disposition, how conflated the mind with useless and overborne conjectures, yet the movement of his notes and the very breeze, the cold breeze, serve to convince us that there is a reality outside of ours. But the bird comes from nowhere and leaves the same, and betrayal, in a tiny moment, filters the whole world through our eyes: the silence becomes noise, the dream falls away from truth, and winter is still so very cold and dreary.

February 10th, 2012

IV. Hardly has a day been significant the whole month, but hardly has that great desire and emotion cast into urgency the minor troubles of life with the deep poetic measure of voice. Vain worries of days innumerable and idleness condemned to unneeded struggles, have ceded to the reflection of new breath, new life--the fatigue and indescribable burdens have gone and I feel once again a man, a poet! Only had the light to project its predestined warmth, only the birds redouble their calls, and the earth once more turn its face up toward the sun, and I have taken hold of that ancient and most renewing notion: it is spring and my heart is alive!

February 28th, 2012

V. In the fields: the day is hazy, warm, no clouds but a gentle breeze at times from the south. The once many green and newly sprouted plants have succumb to the heavy frost, and though the sun is exceedingly bright, back amongst the hedges and within the weeds, there are still patches of it lying concealed, weighing down some unhappy leaf or stem. Whole plants have turned brown and mushy, but some of those same, protected by something I do not know or perceive, whether it be earlier sun or the open air, remain vibrant and seem envied by the frostbitten. The primrose has come through and some of its flowers were part of my lunch--also picked speedwell for tea. Two horses watched as I sat amongst the grass.

Before long we are overwhelmed by ambition and defeated by the very act we thought would free us. This scenery soon vanishes and I am taken up with the complaints for which I came here to be freed. I question my motivation, my understanding, and I see the pale light of the sun as the troubled thoughts with which I make believe poetry is true, not just for me, but as a witness to some unperceived world at large. Be the frost only fatal to those plants, there weighs a heavy silence upon my skin, that had I sprouted amongst these lanes and winding hedges, I would have lost my buds to prematurity, wanting nothing less than I should be the first to feel the sun. But I have retired, or yet have never bloomed, amongst that all too-crowded field, and gather my strength for the coming spring.

March 1st, 2012

VI. It is important to have confidence in a whim--this by which the mind may free itself from habit. Inspiration lies in the decisions we disdain and the ideas we refuse. Intuition gives elegance to action, though it may proceed from an idle brain. Happiness is felt in provoking ourselves, so that whatever we consider displeasure, by the end of the day softens our demeanour, and before long, finds it hard to part ways with. For it seems the character of our thoughts play us a fool: had it never succeeded in humbling us, or showing where we go wrong, or giving us another dimension which to consider, from what could we finally release ourselves and dare a new beginning? I do not mean to say our whims are all agreeable, they

---

gain life through contrariety: 'The world's a scene of changes,' says Cowley, 'and to be constant in nature were inconstancy.'

March 13th, 2012

VII. A fire in an apartment two or three buildings down from us broke out today. I was oblivious to the fact for some time, though the faint smell of smoke and the distant alarm played with my imagination while I occupied myself with the quiet duty of books. It pulled me to other thoughts and reminiscences to muse rather innocently on the origins of that commotion until I got up the curiosity to look out the window. There, just close enough in the courtyard, could I see the black smoke seeping upwards through the parts of a window-frame, and soon, as if the more I looked, the more I became aware of it: the sound of glass shattering, the tar popping and falling from the roof, and the wooden rafters cracking, my mind awakened to the strange horror of the spectacle.

When the devastation does not concern us, we are willing to look with a smile on misfortune and watch as others are picked up or dragged along to their fate; we may touch compassion with a look, but ultimately our hand does not extend past its reach, and whether pity be at our own febrility, or has been entwined in the deep evolution of the human, we always find it a relief to have our own worries and problems than those of anyone else. He who is selfish is worse at hiding this emotion, but he who can hide it finds that what he pities is only as much as what he cannot give, and the man who renounces everything has no need for human sentiment. I do not suppose the fire proved dangerous for anyone; perhaps I shall hear quite offhandedly of the damage, or nothing will be said at all; for it is in our nature to suffer in silence, and in its submission to wail for our loss.

March 15th, 2012

VIII. Anxiety and expectation, left unfulfilled, may still of a fuller and far-seeking reality take hold, wherein lies the instant that we are true to ourselves. To forget of things high and glorious or low and vain, and for no other reason but that we are alive, feel the blood rise into our cheeks, our muscles tense, and in the pure silence of a moment, when it is only us and our imagination that exist, know that we have seen or perceived something which lighter occasion deceives, seems the true bearing of what the Muses call for us poetry. What comes through pain, or the strain of those mental parts, is the idea of ourselves trying to see another world; it asks of us an effort which may only be ground out by separate moments, separate feelings, all concentrated on the same anxious and unexpected outcome. When it is finished, there is only one way that can be seen--doubt vanishes! Humanity reigns in the darkness, but we all too often look outside of ourselves.

March 27th, 2012

IX. One of the saddest and most disappointing things we may consider is to look out upon a land and feel that it is no longer new. An enemy may be appeased; the book that turns boring may be left, but when the trees and the flowers and the slight incline of the hills no longer entice our sight, where can the mind look, or where can our steps wander? I find it somewhat distracting to know that what one day gives inspiration, the next becomes insipid; what at one time is foolish, now is the fashion; if spring is beautiful, winter is grey, and if happiness is the truth of a moment, disappointment is that of the next, and the land may never be renewed but by our long and almost mortal absence.

Sacred ground but seldom exists anymore, and what it is that always keeps our imagination alive, dwindles in respect to the unholy and casual way we displace the things we are searching for. The old stone walls, the mounds, some tall and wide tree, they are sufficient for the eyes, but somewhere fall short in the mind when we know too much about them. Ignorance strays not far from intuition, and truth has but a small life to fill--for if the land were ever new would we concede to its vision.

Today, the new spring offers me nothing, and I wonder if I have not sapped the fair beauty of my imagination.

March 29th, 2012

X. Spirit is the consummation of experience. The more I find myself willing to give worth to what I have done or where I have been, the less I feel in need of straying far and wide, and demanding of others what they think. There is built in us a structure like that of a plant which slowly heaves and exhales with the sunlight and the shade; for may it run vigorous to the source of its ideas, the thoughts with which it is fed will produce pale leaves or vibrant flowers regardless of the care that it is given. There are wildflowers that grow firmly and stick fast in the mind and accompany us into our adult life and always be the fragrant scents by which we stroll, and may we choose kindly and pick of them daily, still may we neglect of their proper essence.

There was a man, I heard, who cared not for the craze, or what was current in the news, and yet he lived discredited in society. When asked what he thought of those popular topics of the time, a strange indifference came over him, of which many interpreted as ignorance, but being urged moreover to finally say something, he spoke of what affected him immediately, and after speaking all of this, they replied, 'But you have said nothing that concerns the subject,' and turned angrily from him. From the moment we become molested by something that we have not experienced first-hand, by something that we have not given actively to in our daily lives, our spirit waivers; everything outside of its grasp, or outside of its will to receive, is meant to fulfill and popularize the affair or the issue with which it deals. The spirit is crushed by the importance of popularity, and what we begin to experience from it be nourishment for those by whom it was created.

March 30th, 2012

XI. I believe spring brings to us new endeavors which are not entirely our own. Only so many times can we look out the window at the bright sun before we are inspired by something that cold and quiet reflection had hidden. It is not that we have called forth some urge or hidden desire, but have been summoned to some enterprising task the beginning and end of which has a common but indefinable link with the odours of new blossoms and the green leaf. To one in spring-time, his fears are often fulfilled not by what habitually scares him, but by the idea that he may miss out on the plenitude of the experience--he cares only for his emotions, the rest is not for him to be burdened with. I parch corn, pick herbs, and eat weeds; for these are more than just efforts and small sustenance, but symbolic of inner conquest, whereupon the strength and creativity of the mind depend--he who knows not the taste of these things, knows not the virtue of his thought; and all of this, in the end, culminates in the expression of new ideas.

March 31st, 2012

XII. There is nothing we do not cease questioning unless it be phenomena, but in those inquiries illusion no longer holds a serious part of the explanation--we laugh at it and amuse ourselves with the unexplainable, but our scientific minds demand fact. There was a time when all truth was attributed to the direct consequence of habit, or retribution for a deed left unnoticed, but this has ceded place to the much less remarkable and much more dull idea of circumstance: what happens to me is bound to happen because the outcome exists somewhere in the world. There is still a desire to see into the secrets of the universe and the human mind, but we more regularly demand of them a cause.

Some months ago I came upon a solitary raspberry-bush growing alone next to a trickling creek, and began to think of the causes which had brought it to this spot, and thought of the germination of seeds and their propagation by birds. However, after a few uneasy moments, this no longer sufficed and I became open to the possibility that that spot may have been home to an old habitation and quaint garden. But then, even more prevalent in my mind, was the idea that a traveling worker a few decades ago had come to the surrounding orchards to find work, and taking up this shaded spot by the creek, ate his wild and hard-earned lunch, letting fall a few berries he had picked from a road-side garden. Or perhaps the planting was intentional and a pair of newlyweds had placed it there as a marker to their old meeting-grounds. Or it had been planted over a dead body; or had sprouted from a seed in the stomach of a dead body whose last meal were the last fruits of summer.

The mind works and is cultivated by illusion--it desires what is unanswerable; the only harm lies in being illusive to our own identity, in making up facts so as to avoid the problem. I do not mean to say ignorance would create an eternal bliss, for it is the ridding of this ignorance that will take us past the dull sobriety of our world, but that naivety, and the unceasing possibility of humanity and spirituality can produce in us a truer meaning to the facts of life.

April 8th, 2012

XIII. It is quite current in our day to hear that we must learn from the mistakes of the past; for it seems the past offers us nothing to be learned except rectification. When sitting down at my desk, I find that whatever we call the faults of the past are not something from which I learn a great deal because they are not so easily detectable in the present. Truly, the past comes to us through so many strange and awkward moods that, like Thoreau in his description of the ants, men shall run around as viciously as insects before they realize that there is no measure to the past unless it is every possibility of the present.

There are many sensible of this idea

who have said that the past lives in us daily, that one day is sufficient for the end and the beginning of the universe, but to human affairs this is much less understandable. We frown to hear that the flower was not always a flower, that rocks have been formed by rain, and the world, if it ended tomorrow, or has already ended, no sure escape for the human. Our existence becomes a blank and terrible dissolution, a mere condition of the atmosphere and its reaction to light, yet it is from this that we learn. For I know that if I ever accomplish anything great, or anything worth exception to anyone else but myself, that in the future it will not be anything to be learned from, but will be, for whom or whatever sits or walks in a meadow on a hot day, a gentle cooling breeze, or the first rain-drops of a coming storm; it will perhaps be a flower growing upon the mountain heights, or the sediment flowing in a muddy creek, but in the end it will be a particle of the blank night; and that, really, is the only thing it needs to be.

April 10th, 2012

XIV. Let us note the ages of our lives, not merely the passive turnings of the year, but that wherein our spirit grows. This is something particular and so quickly forgotten that before we believe ourselves to have mastered some language, finished some book, or enjoyed the notes of a music we never thought could exist, we consider them normal aspects of our being and see no growth in our hearts except what we are forced to believe of culture and society. We are admitted into the true depths of light and perception only when the constraining force of our attitude cedes to an alternative outside of itself; and only does the warmth and consciousness of mind exceed our physical parts when it sees languor and strife turn itself to motivation. All of this is lost if we know not in what hour of what day, or within what age, we first looked up to the stars and felt betrayed; all atrophies until the final hour if we have not felt a word upon us exhale its ray of sun. We must look into our lives and urge advantage; we must see that we are not merely fodder for time, but permeate through one lone and lonesome world a thought, which for so many an age, has already passed into the dark.

April 17th, 2012

XV. To breathe the open air! I feel of the past and ancient, and how strange that when I think of it, I am not bound a victim of the same old sort of daily life, but am at liberty from reason, free of the past, and feel utterly content that the future, and each evolving moment in life, holds the fullest realization of thought. How soon the winds die down on stormy days, and how clear the light within a gloomy sky! It suffices that we speak one word correctly in any given moment and our perception changes; one gesture to feel a fuller connection with the spiritual world, and but a little verse to elect himself king of his own conscience. This is the joy of finishing a poem.

April 23rd, 2012

XVI. Man may out of his greatest failure succeed and turn the course of Nature unto his liking. He is never so old that his thoughts cannot be young but always too young to consider himself complete, and the time comes when he bows to the possibility that he is not alone and anything greater seems a task for which the silent workings of his mind were not conceived. Yet none are so great as to encompass all, and few are so small as to believe themselves unworthy. Thus, the practice of stealing away into the lone and ancient myths upon which fear, envy, spite, and jealousy, hinge themselves, are perforations into the finer fabric of the soul, for which it more often injures than heals. And if ever better silk be attained, that certain material with which is made the threadbare of his garments must extend past the simple make-up of his accepted universe. For he is never more at home than when he enters those places wherein familiarity seeks not a friend.

April 24th, 2012

XVII. I was sitting at my desk this dreary morning with the window barely open, not even enough to hear the rain, when the faint odor of a summer field came over me. My plans were to go to the country today and walk, and though the misfortune was not so great when I arose and found the day unfit to my adventure, yet this fragrant smell that passed through the window immediately gave me longings to be in Mornant. However, the oddest part of it was that my brooding quickly began to fade and the more I indulged in this felicitous smell, the more I felt as if I were among a thick grass that, by the summer's heat, had already started to dry up and brown--yarrow, mallow, and cinquefoil were spread amongst it. I remember it: a field of wheat was not far, or had been recently harvested, and as I looked over an ancient stone wall to a stone granary that seemed of the Middle Ages, with the white sky trailing the landscape off to the horizon in a haze, this image, along with the smell, transported me to a time, which when young, caused me to think that such places I would never actually see. Here my boyish fascinations had found reality, and now that I could see them, far from my native home, I began to wonder if it were not this smell of summer fields at the origin of my youth and my displacement to find that which makes one feel at home. And will it not be this field and stone wall in Mornant that tell me in old age the reason for which manhood has begun its search for still more distant and more secluded retreats?

May 8th, 2012

XVIII. How easy it is to accept the word of another, I have been at pains to convince myself, whether out of respect, or somewhat for the hidden motives which they entail, but not indeed for the quality of the discussion, or the truth of their thoughts, to wager anything greater in friendship or kindness. To relate and tell another of our day, even in the simplest discussion, I find to be wearisome, awkward, and feel it not from a genuine sentiment of interaction that it is said, but from the intent of the person to gratify his need for power. This is, of course, no magic rule and fits in to no single profile more than any other, but is the long and worn-out strand by which society finds acceptance in experience. Yet it happens thus that we relate to win, to gain, to find that which our companion has not done, but stop short of that which the relation may dispose us towards. So we hold out our hands that someone may take hold of them, but lest that person is willing to be led, we let go just as quickly, to despise or be despised--and it is this by which our daily lives are guided!

I care not for the common run of events, but as well, truth without the experience to withdraw from the mere pedantic is ever so foreign and too heavy for me to bear. I would like to speak something full every time I have someone's attention, but how foolishly would they look upon me if I did not ask of them the same sensations that they ask of me--it is life, it is nature, but it is not my will to power.

May 16th, 2012

XIX. Once innocence is lost in that in which it was believed to abide, and where the unabounding smile made us feel looked upon as the holder and journeyman of life, from which the knowledge of things could be pulled, once this is lost, I say, and there arises before us someone or something that is not so easily conceived, is it fear, or is it pity, that we should feel, knowing that we had had a hand in its formation? Or should we be proud, aware that a part of us resides externally and that something of our innermost being seems touching the surface upon which its actions and manners are born? Or is it something forever lost, something that in the far-off horizon of our thoughts, does not flee us, but is the ever-enduring consummation of the present, that part which is given us upon our waking into this world, and that part which never wholly finds each individual human? It is an opening, a turning towards, that if it see past the reality it has awaken to, must from the moment it begins to see, blind itself to all the conceptions with which this world is forthwith governed. Whether it is a turning away, or an analysis, it is an intonation towards perspective. It is lost so easily, that even before our first self-inspired thought exists, we have given place to what our culture demands.

May 30th, 2012

XX. During those moments of oncoming sleep, when the solemn hours of the night show the world in its deepest origins, more than once has a terrible uneasiness come upon me. A sudden rush, proceeding from the realization of some eternal and defining moment, not in my life, but to the universe as a whole, arrives through the darkness of my eyes and opens the fullest depths of imagination to a strong and unrelenting purpose. Since childhood, though with age it has become more distant, the same question has always been connected with this experience, and it has always befuddled me.

Will we ever come to know ourselves again in this reality in which we are always becoming? It is too easy to believe the human race perpetual and immediate to this world, and necessary before all other things, and that which is lost, forever placed within something anew: but what if the traces of those ancient tribes of our ancestors still hold the stock, not of our physical and daily lives, but of our mental and capricious whims?

Energy itself, being always present, has somehow formed within the confines of this air our body, and the power of man, created by this universe, oversteps and thrusts himself into that energy--or renewal of energy--every time he puts to work his intellectual and imaginative faculties, so that all anterior knowledge and spirituality become individually posterior. If this power is supplied by the loss of all other ideas in the world, is it safe to imagine that fate is the ratio wherein the loss of those ideas is not enough to renew the increase of our mental powers? But as this energy is renewed and foreseen by whatever action or power we create, we are indebted not by the weight of that energy--the annihilating power of fate--nor the good or the evil that it may bring upon us, but by the loss to recreate, or re-stimulate, ourselves again to that temptation, or fugitive mode of thinking, until a certain amount of time has passed, and which perhaps may never be humanly possible to compensate for again.

This, indeed, is what I find myself contemplating sometimes; and last night, this uneasiness coming upon me, for the first time in all my years of existence I realized that humanity is neither necessary to this world, and that if the human race one day becomes no more, the renewal of energy of which I have been speaking, will no longer turn its powers upon our intellectual force. But that means there is an intonation of dimension in us, and if there be something of the eternal, like this energy, then it is a part of eternity itself. But can we really reflect upon the eternal movement which makes up the loss of that creative force once started in another world, or by another people? If the power of the past elaborates into idea this renewing energy, human sentiment, the imagination, the words with which we describe our actions, and the poetic mode of thinking, are the smoke of a blazing fire kindled in the anterior realms of our consciousness, and as our perceptions lighten and darken, as we see, not through the window, but the reflection that window provides, so we begin to feel that eternal, renewing force; it is no longer in the future or the past, it is rather only dependent upon the human for existence, but existing independent of us; it is we who have become the necessary part of something that has not necessity in it. In this way, our place in this world becomes the seat of eternity, and though we no longer seek out the cave for shelter, no longer chase the animal through the woods, or beat upon the hides our recurring traditions, the renewal of that energy has already forged them into a path in our perceptions. We merely walk down the hall, or pick up a pen, or speak to someone in the street, and there is that loss, that fate, that prevents us from finally seeing that we have walked out of our cave, have killed the animal we were chasing, and have reached the end of our song.

June 18th, 2012

XXI. There is a value we place upon objects, above their merit, solely because of the occult property that lies within them. The significance of a book or an artifact, a pair of shoes or a shirt, mean little to us daily, but when we look upon them, or think of the pleasure that they have at one time given us, or will give us, we experience a higher sublimity that bonds them to the physical part of life, so that we feel them as a product of our own imagination. It is normal for us to care and take things under our wing; for us to bestow upon the inanimate a cause for existence, and even to believe that we have given life to something without which would have never been, yet it is not merely ourselves that we are looking for in those things, but the faint traces of a long lost divinity. The prize that is the object we take in hand is forever a search for something we know not how to define, nor believe to reside within us: it is the holding of a thought within our hands that creates the perception of our belief.

Yet there is still something omnipresent and malleable, and whether from outward appearance, or the solitary intuition of inner life, the object we had once prized, again turns to nothing and finally falls away from sentiment. Before we know it we have lost interest or we have found something new, and the cold and indifferent way we look back upon it, tells us of the strange interpretation we have made thus far. Those plants I was first able to identify, and felt could never gather enough of in the field, I now pass by; I look at them and know them, but spare my efforts. The trail importunes me to leave them, but they in turn ask me to grow, for our existence relies upon the recognition of what we believe in, and just how much the object is necessary to our interior being is how much less we are willing to proceed unto those things we cannot put our hands on.

July 5th, 2012

XXII.   Every   new   venture   is   the explanation of an intention that tries to live and receive the promise of its hope, and it is thus by the long and idle turning of repetition that we find our way. Habit, whether it is the light by which we find a haven safe and secure, never to test its limits again, already demands of us a task that has not yet received its beginning. For the further it seems I travel in time and gather those years   about   me   with   the   same indifference that they fall away, the further I try to exact some greater and enduring presence which remunerates with   pride   what   is   left   before   me unfinished, given momentum only by the unity of my habits. Those of you, then, who look upon new lands and supplant the stable vision of life with the desert of blind and overrunning darkness, know that I too have sought out my haven, and I too live in the grips of the strongest repetition. But the somber and profound thought which enriches the life of a lost and helpless voyager is that, what remains from that which we have passed on from, has already started on a path to meet us again.

August 12th, 2012

XXIII. There are times when even Shakespeare presents a heaviness and whether we are much inclined to wander through those realms of imagination, the door must be sat beside and remain locked. Desire and volition can force no fantasy of their own that does not soon die and become forgettable. To live, they need the silent breath of imagination; they need a reaction to nature to remunerate themselves, but this cannot by our own hearts be decreed. We are all unstable without recourse to our own form of creation; away from it, we are ever malleable to an outside force; our desires become a frenzy, our will a vice. Who, then, that finds himself alone in this struggle, will see that just as he flees, a reconciliation begins--but how far today is the silence of a god. I work past poems and essays with but a word and cull no sublimity from their ideas. Time feels in itself lost and remains on the surface of a thought.

August 23rd, 2012

XXIV. Picked blackberries yesterday and last week--made blackberry juice and patted some into cakes to dry as the Indians did of old. There is no reality, of course, and we are ever side by side with those things we think are far. The fruit stains the hand as it is picked, just as it did to those who were buried in the bogs of the northern countries when they ate of them for a last meal. What is strange to wonder, though, is if that same sustenance which falls to the earth has fooled our hearts into believing that what is lost can always be found in something else. For we have so often found what we are looking for that it no longer takes the name of interest, and what is genuine is only another word for what we have already understood. What I mean is, the veil of perception and reality coexist in the object: the same time I pick the berry and take it back home for my meal is the same time many years ago someone picked those same berries for the last meal of that man or women who was sacrificed in a bog--I go off to the sacrifice, but live on through the belief that causes their sacrifice. And yet we must still ask ourselves: would I exist if the berry did not? Our actions contain the great mystery that is the past and the future.

September 1st, 2012

XXV. Those meditations with which we extend the mind must be so far removed from daily life that sometimes days and hours will pass before one fresh thought comes upon us. The strain of living in communion with anticipation, with waiting, with rushing, is a life wherein poetry cannot breathe, but are nonetheless the qualities which we impose upon ourselves to reach that frozen plain of myth wherein the mystery of being resides unforgettable.

I do not know if solitude is such that it may take away all care, for at the base of all that is detestable is the image of ourselves fleeing into the delusions of heroic qualities. There is a clarity that remains exempt however, one that is entered into merely, and not produced. What I speak of is poetry in its most undetailed form, that of which exists without us and raises in and out of the thick gaseous clouds of the universe, creating at once stars and galaxies and the dark matter that floats unnoticed before our eyes; and when we try to put our hands on it and make it comprehensible, though the inspiration may still be evident, we turn from it in disgust or boredom because it is once again this thing that is detestable, that covers everything we touch, and is at bottom the essence of the human. We do not want to know our nature, but want to give to it a poetry that speaks only of ourselves, and if there is something of sublimity to be reached through these words that we have created for our own understanding, then it stands not in the human, but in the capricious traditions that the human has made; for the whole weight of the past must sit upon us so that we may walk lightly into the evening.

September 3rd, 2012

XXVI. When the evening drifts away to night how pleasant to be overcome by the trivialities of the day, attentive to the very charms of fatigue, and the slumber of the mind, as it hesitates upon its way to the netherworlds of sleep. In those moments when we expect nothing, and are neither pulled with the chains of tomorrow, and have soothed our burdened conscience by the extenuation of fault, the void upon which our senses are released, finds itself a place of rest on those dearest, and at times, most common features of nature.

It happened that a flock of migrating cranes passed by the open window, and the moment they became fixed in my eye was almost the same as if a dream had passed over my clouded thoughts; for there was at once my gaze upon the night sky, and at another the strange flash of some deeper image within it, reflected only by the faint light that rose up from the street. In an instant I went out to look more closely, and the silence, and the faint agitation of their wings, foretold a presence to none but the luckiest glance--their call, their chant even, shrouded them in some mystery I knew not. The buffalo and the elk have given their paths to men as a means to travel, but has not the bird, in its migration, given us a means for religion? For the few seconds of their passage, I was a follower of a ritual in the sky. Where are they now? Have they passed the fertile plains of the Rioja? Or have they gained the stifling heat of Andalucia? As I slept, they with some undefined urge, passed the very regions that I had turned from, and so light as to float upon the air without a worry. I want not to know any mystery of the earth than to be initiated into the realm of its existence, and wonder if this would not be a symbol for the ways that succeed in the ground of thought.

September 7th, 2012

XXVII. I have tasted acorns recently and find it hard to acknowledge their superiority among nuts, even with the bitterness taken out of them. But when one knows of refinement, how difficult it is to suffer for insignificance and to defend the tastes of the past when closer to our hearts there grows the need for something more familiar. It is even difficult to suppose that we are guided by extreme or unique choices when there is a longing to accept that which has become so common. Thoreau had noted this phenomenon long ago, but for apples, saying that he believed there were only some that could be eaten outside, away from the place called home, and being brought in among our familiar surroundings, lost their taste or were too hard for the appetite to digest.

There is a life, then, that is lived beyond our immediate experience, and like the wild apple, must be tasted out in the field, far away from home. It is the minor vision of a world that is always looking the other way, which is soon to follow the direction of those eyes that have made so common for us the mountains and hills we knew not yet existed. What, then, is satisfying? What makes us taste of something so dull and inedible as the acorn? It is not the shallow look of curiosity, but the idea of finding something that will reveal to us the reality of survival, that has such a hard mutability we push it away before we have even taken off our portion--it is the idea of being initiated into the mystery of the earth. And, then, with

---

what joy could we experience the end!

September 9th, 2012

XXVIII. A flock of cranes flew over again this morning, this time in the dark, echoing in the low cloudy sky, but taking a path to the northward instead. If we could only veer from ourselves so easily, but migration itself is only meant to go two ways. We must ask ourselves, then, that when we get there, will we pick ourselves up and return.

September 19th, 2012

XXIX. It is not long before the thing we reflect on cedes itself to the near past wherein yesterday or two weeks ago our real attention lies. There lies behind the simplest object a reason, and the mind seems more willing to recede to it than force itself upon the unknown, which is why, so often, concentration is one of the flimsiest undertakings. Thus, there is reason I cannot sit in peaceful ease today: my fear of the past and the deep, sprawling abyss, that comes close to me.

September 22nd, 2012

XXX. Hiking yesterday; the day was gray, autumn-like, with a heavy wind from the south. The ferns are rusting away and from the valleys there breathes out upon the hills the changing colour of the leaves. Collected chestnuts and hazelnuts, but the latter are quite worthless, while the others give a feeling of ambition, and so we are making chestnut cream.

Descending the trail earlier, a tree fell before us on the other side--for the countless times that trees are seen lying on the ground, it is a rare and special occurrence to hear one fall of its own. This is only the second time in my life that I have been so close to feel the terror and wonder of it all, and the only time I was able to walk up to it after the fact. Not but three days ago I found the wing of a finch lying well off the trail near a bush.

There was a strange phenomenon in the sky yesterday of which I must speak: as the sun was setting, there were rays of light off to the east as if another sun was going to rise. For a moment, it seemed two suns existed, and morning and evening were one, and this persisted for so long, that were we to have lain our tasks aside, we might have found ourselves waking from stubborn sleep.

September 24th, 2012

XXXI. To be heroic in this world, one must be prepared to ask, 'What if?' And the answer that he shall always receive will be, 'Either... Or...' However, I do not mean this to sound as if one must take his lessons directly from the philosopher's mouth; I rather mean that his decision should not escape him in that vital moment. Nor should this be taken all the way to the extreme of single-mindedness, lest the mountain feel its own avalanche and not stand firm enough against it. Thus, the inheritance of our whole future comes with a sign over it that says: know thyself. But the currency of this expression is no longer the reason for which we rise from bed, so that our curiosity has given up on the abstract, and only where we see the light will we let ourselves be guided. What was for us once a question is now an answer wherefrom we move away and cry out in longing, 'What if?'

September 29th, 2012

XXXII. What is it that we conceal when we look towards an ideal moment? What appears to us comes as part of a world that we can only vaguely conceive, but one in which we imagine a whole set of circumstances, accomplishing this or that with greater or lesser conviction, until we arrive at some culminating point where perfection is grasped for just a moment. And yet we know that if something perfect must exist it is only because imperfection exists and the whole way unto the ideal a series of sufferings. But we must not consider through all our pains there will bloom within us an everlasting peace; for just as a door and four walls may lead us to expect shelter, the rain may still come in. When it happens though, when we find entrance into a warm and inviting home, the essence of that ideal is always hard to grasp and we despair over the contrast of perception and imagination, only to turn upon that thing that was always concealed within us and within the event. It is still an illusion, but in order to feel it, we must be led away, and to ever know it, we must return.

October 2nd, 2012

XXXIII. That which is unique seems all the more to make what is around us less so that we forget the whole circumstance leans solely on the force of our own interpretation.

While having dinner last night, just at the moment that I happened to look up, a greenish-blue ball of light flew across the tiny part of sky that our window encloses; but from that moment, until I spoke of the object only a few seconds later, did a confidence steadily grow in my disparaged and up until then unsure attempts in writing, that everything thought childish in my life, in that instant became truth, and whatever I would do from here on would not lead me astray whether I doubted or not. It was a coincidence that touched something I had hardly ever seen; it was not a revelation, nor did I think some divine presence involved in it, but it was the circumstance that bade the whole realm of possibility, the whole realm of existence, mutual to my own poor and daily life. Superiority and the hierarchy of individuals, and of ideas, are merely the games of men, whereas the quiet look into a truthful world beholds the unique aim of his being.

October 3rd, 2012

XXXIV. A large group of cranes pass over.

There is something so bland in life that we become subverse to the very details that make it up; and yet, brought to our attention, those details are of no special concern, though they have created our interest in the first place. When we ask someone to stand out, we are not asking of anything genuine or long-standing, but merely a blind antagonist to draw us in to an ever greater competition of self-worth. But how foolish! For he who is willing to combat his fellow-man proves he is not on even terms with him and has not attained the superiority of triumph in his own mind. Instead of the ideas of excellence that another puts forth, should he find the terms for his own conviction. But if there is a sage of dire consequence, he has folded up his robe, for among the vast infinitude of prophecy there are but one or two decisions to be made. Perhaps we could still hear his echo if it were not that he too has become so bland.

October 11th, 2012

XXXV. The 27th was the first day of autumn--a faint chill and pelting rain; the trees taking on different colours, the ferns rusting away. One day we wake up and it is spring, another winter; for we call the first of things pure: the first taste, the first scent; but the first expression of autumn, the first realization that our earth is moving further away from the sun, in that thought alone there is the greatest solitude and the greatest expression of thought.

Daily life has a great warming effect to it--it is wonderful to be caught up in our habits and see from within the season changing. Haste, anxiety, and dread, all take on new meanings, those of which we can recede into and find relief in the fact that our own storms and our own frailties are matters less eternal than the wind. It is even soothing to rediscover a pressing need and find that the importance given to it was but an illusion caused by the summer months or the full moon. The way we feel a certain look, the way we take someone's word, are all open to the many interpretations among which only one may please us, and we stand to it with a deeply embedded conviction. It is good to have opinions, but when the seasons change and the snowflakes fall, let them travel into that furthest solitude, and only then, let us see what comes back to us.

October 29th, 2012

XXXVI. The sky is overcast and somehow the more beautiful for it. The resurgence of something, at one time held in the light, gains the absolute clearest perspective when it can be approached on cloudy days. It is not that we see anything new, rather it is the coming into contradiction of our own perception. In that way, what was held of interest once before, now finds conflict with how we must approach it. This is true for the way we read books, listen to music, and try to figure out the tasks of our day, and this is also true of any solution: how much light an object receives is ultimately the basis for our perception.

The lake is deeper with the loss of light,

---

the forest more silent; animals step with an approaching calm, and it is all too easy to forget that we must function with the rising of the sun. The trees have gone from light yellow to dark red in the matter of a week and it is with renewed interest that I take up the terrifying banalities of life.

November 7th, 2012

XXXVII. Hiked on the 10th; mushroom hunting and the first Cepe de Bordeaux I've ever found. Those places where the mushroom lives and sprouts up are enchanting: they are on the most unnoticeable part of ground and give importance to a spot that we would not have noticed in any other circumstance. To search for them is perhaps a meditation on nature; the robin, the squirrel, and even the deer are apt to cross our path, and still other birds, or the tracks of unknown animals, and though the mushroom sits in the back of our mind, we anticipate an encounter with something far less known. Thus, going into the underbrush, or pushing aside dead leaves, enlightens a conscious courage that is almost as ancient as it is foreign to our daily lives. Certainly he who finds what he's been looking for has always been searching for something else.

November 15th, 2012

About the Author

Douglas Thornton is a poet living in France. He has published a book of poetry (Woodland Poems) and currently has a website: www.fromapoet.com.

* 9 7 8 2 9 5 6 6 8 5 5 0 0 *